FIRST AMERICANS

The Chumash

TERRY ALLAN HICKS

mc Marshall Cavendish
Benchmark
New York

ACKNOWLEDGMENTS

For Jamie, who likes tales of the Beforetime at bedtime

Series consultant: Raymond Bial

Marshall Cavendish Benchmark
99 White Plains Road
Tarrytown, New York 10591-9001
www.marshallcavendish.us

Text, maps, and illustrations copyright © 2008 by Marshall Cavendish Corporation
Map and illustration by Rodica Prato
Craft illustrations by Chris Santoro

Library of Congress Cataloging-in-Publication Data
Hicks, Terry Allan.
The Chumash / by Terry Allan Hicks.
p. cm. — (First Americans)
Summary: "Provides comprehensive information on the background, lifestyle, beliefs, and present-day lives of the Chumash people"—Provided by publisher.
Includes bibliographical references and index.
ISBN-13: 978-0-7614-2678-3
1. Chumash Indians—Juvenile literature. I. Title. II. Series.
E99.C815H52 2007
979.4004'9758—dc22
2006034101

Front cover: A Chumash girl wears a headband made of seashells.
Title page: A collection of Chumash rattles
Photo research by: Connie Gardner
Cover photo by Marilyn "Angel" Wynn/Nativestock.com
The photographs in this book are used by permission and through the courtesy of: Nativestock.com: Marilyn "Angel" Wynn, 1, 4, 9, 10, 11, 12, 14, 16, 17, 19, 20, 28, 30, 32, 35, 37; Corbis: Nik Wheeler, 7; Jim Zuckerman, 8; Daniel J. Cox, 24; David Muench, 27, 33; Dembinsky Photo Associates: 38.

Editor: Deborah Grahame
Publisher: Michelle Bisson
Art Director: Anahid Hamparian
Series Designer: Symon Chow

Printed in China
3 5 6 4 2

CONTENTS

1 · WHO ARE THE CHUMASH?

Native Americans have lived along the California coast, close to the Pacific Ocean, for thousands of years. Yet very few of California's native peoples have chosen to hunt, fish, or travel on the open ocean. One people who did venture out onto the ocean were the Chumash (CHOO-mash).

The Chumash lived in a seven-thousand-square-mile (eighteen-thousand-square-kilometer) area of what is now southern California. Their territory stretched from present-day San Luis Obispo in the north to Malibu in the south, and as far inland as the Santa Monica Mountains. They also lived on four of the Channel Islands—Anacapa, Santa Cruz, San Miguel, and Santa Rosa—that lie thirty miles (forty-eight km) offshore, across the Santa Barbara Channel.

To reach the islands, the Chumash built huge wooden

The Pacific Ocean at Point Conception, on the California coast

A map of Chumash territory, showing its location in present-day California

canoes called tomols. They paddled their tomols far out to sea and up and down the coast, trading with neighboring peoples using beads made out of seashells. In fact, the word *Chumash* probably means "makers of shell bead money" in the language of one of these peoples.

All Native Americans are descended from people who **migrated** from Asia more than 20,000 years ago across a "land bridge" that once connected Siberia and Alaska. As early as 13,000 BCE, **Paleo-Indians** were living along the Pacific Coast in what is now California. By 3000

Anacapa Island—actually a chain of three smaller islands—was home to the Chumash for thousands of years.

The Rainbow Bridge

The Chumash believe their story began on Santa Cruz Island, when the spirit Hutash built a "rainbow bridge" —called *Wishtoyo* in the Chumash language—so the Chumash could cross to the mainland. Some of the Chumash fell off the bridge into the ocean, but Hutash saved them by turning them into dolphins. To this day, the Chumash say the dolphins are their brothers and sisters.

Some tomols were made from the reeds that grow along the southern California coast.

BCE, some of these people had become the **Proto-Chumash**. We know very little about them, but they were probably hunter-gatherers who ate land and sea animals and wild seeds and berries.

By about 500 CE, the Chumash had developed one of the most advanced cultures on the California coast. They hunted with bows and arrows, fished with both hooks and nets, and made beautiful, tightly woven reed baskets. Different groups of Chumash had their own hunting and fishing grounds, their own dialects of the Chumash language, and their own traditions.

When the first Spanish explorers arrived in California in 1542, there may have been as many as 20,000 Chumash liv-

The Chumash used clam shells for buttons and olivella shells as money.

ing in about 150 villages along the coast and in the mountains. The Spanish claimed all of California as their own, but they did not occupy this territory for many years. In 1769 they began to build religious outposts called missions. The Catholic priests who ran the missions forced the Chumash and other Native Americans to leave their villages, give up their languages and religions, and work on mission farms almost as

Chumash baskets were not only beautiful, but also very useful.

This painting shows a group of Chumash with a Catholic priest at a California mission.

slaves. Those who refused or tried to run away were beaten and sometimes killed. Many Chumash also died from diseases, such as measles, because they had no resistance to them.

By 1833 Mexico—which then included California—became independent from Spain, and the Mexican government took control of the missions. The period of Mexican rule was probably the worst in the history of the Chumash. Some historians believe that hard work, violence, and disease may have killed 60 percent of the Chumash during this time.

California became part of the United States in 1848, but life did not get easier for the Chumash. Many new settlers were now arriving from the east, driving the Chumash off their lands. By 1900 as few as two hundred Chumash were left. It seemed that they and their way of life might disappear forever.

2 · LIFE ON THE CALIFORNIA COAST

Before the Spanish arrived, most Chumash lived in small villages of fifty or more inhabitants. A Chumash village was a cluster of dome-shaped houses called **'aps**. An 'ap was usually twelve to eighteen feet (three-and-a-half to five-and-a-half meters) wide. It was built by sticking willow branches in the ground in a circle, then bending them inward and binding them together to form a dome. The dome was then covered with tule grass, with a hole in the center to let out smoke from cooking fires. Some entrance frames were made of whalebone. Several families usually shared an 'ap, sleeping on raised platforms with storage space underneath.

The village also had a **temescal** as well as a storehouse for food and a playing field. The Chumash loved sports, especially **tikauwich**, a game that was

The temescal, or sweat lodge, was used for Chumash "purification" rites and baths.

The Chumash used weapons and tools like these for hunting and fishing.

something like field hockey.

The village was ruled by a wot, or **hereditary** chief. This person—usually a man, but sometimes a woman—made all the important decisions about village life. The wot settled any disagreements among the Chumash, especially arguments over hunting and fishing grounds.

Chumash life was centered on the search for food, which went on all year long. Men with bows and arrows and spears went high into the mountains to hunt land animals—everything from rabbits and wild birds to deer, elk, and bear. The Chumash also went far out on the Pacific Ocean in their tomols to hunt sea animals such as seals and whales, and to look for fish, including tuna and sharks.

In this painting, a group of Chumash launch a tomol into the Pacific surf.

Berry Jam

The Chumash gathered many types of wild berries for use both as food and as medicine. This easy-to-make jam is full of flavor, and you can make it with blackberries, gooseberries, loganberries, or raspberries. The mixture is very hot while it is cooking, so make sure you have an adult to help you use the stove. You will need these ingredients:

- 2 quarts berries
- 6 cups sugar
- 1 cup vinegar
- large saucepan
- jars with covers

Crush the berries, then combine them with the sugar and vinegar in a large saucepan. Slowly bring the mixture to a boil over medium heat, stirring occasionally. Once the sugar has dissolved, cook the mixture until it thickens. Then, while it is still hot, pour it into jars and cover.

A traditional Chumash boat, made from planks of redwood trees

A tomol could be as long as thirty feet (nine m)—big enough to carry ten people and four thousand pounds (eighteen hundred kilograms) of cargo. The Chumash built tomols by cutting redwood into planks, gluing the planks together with pine tar, and then sanding the surface smooth with sharkskin.

The Chumash ate acorns — often mashed, as shown here — and many different kinds of berries.

The Chumash also gathered shellfish—especially clams, mussels, and abalone—and wild seeds, pine nuts, and berries. When autumn came, entire villages worked together to gather acorns, which were the most important food source for most of California's Native Americans. The Chumash ground up or mashed the acorns, then used them to make porridge, cakes, or fry bread.

The Chumash's neighbors and the Spanish admired Chumash crafts. The Chumash carved beautiful bowls out of **steatite** from the Channel Islands. They were also skilled basket-makers, weaving dried **tule** reeds together to weave baskets so tightly that they could be used for carrying water and even for cooking. Today, Chumash baskets can be found in museums all over the world.

Make a Basket

The Chumash used tule to make their beautiful woven baskets. Why not try making your own basket, using simple materials that should be easy to find where you live?

You will need:

* two 6-yard (5.5-m) lengths of twisted craft paper (available at craft stores)
* scissors
* a ruler

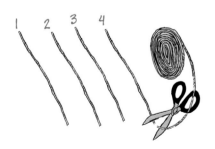

1· Using the scissors and ruler, cut three pieces—each 2 feet (61 centimeters) long—from one of the lengths of twisted craft paper. (You may want to ask an adult to help with the measuring and cutting.)

2· Tie two of the pieces together in the middle with the third piece, using a loose knot. Then cut another piece, 1 foot (30 cm) long, from the paper left over from the same length of twisted craft paper, and push it through the knot you made. Spread the pieces out evenly to form the "ribs" of the basket.

3· Take the second 6-yard (5.5-m) length of twisted craft paper, push it through the loose knot you made, then tighten the knot.

4· Weave the twisted craft paper tightly around the ribs, over one, then under the next, and so on. Keep the layers as close together as possible.

5· When only about 4 inches (10 cm) of twisted craft paper is left, twist the loose end together with the closest rib. Bend the joined piece down to the edge of the basket, then do the same with all the other ribs. Tuck any loose ends under the rim of the basket.

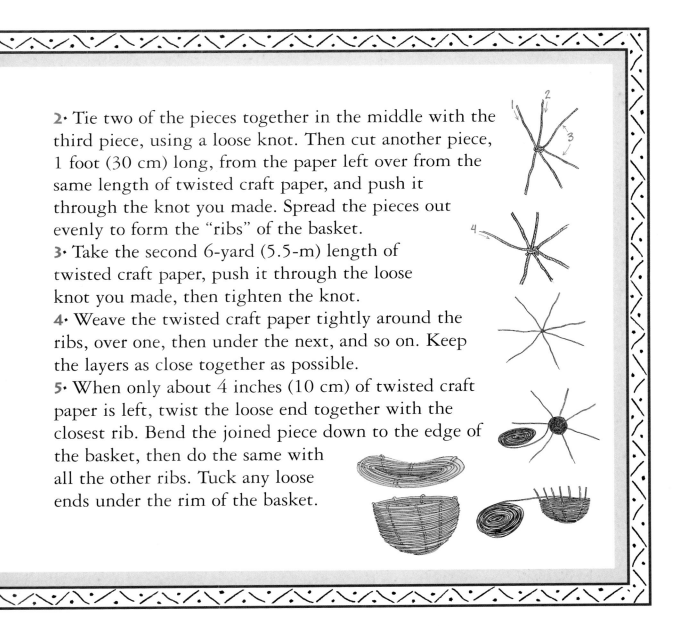

3 · CHUMASH BELIEFS

The Chumash believed there were three worlds, not just the one in which they lived. High above them was the sky world, which was carried by a giant eagle whose beating wings caused the changing phases of the moon. Deep below the earth was another world, held up on the backs of two huge serpents that caused earthquakes when they moved. In between was the world where human beings lived.

All three of the Chumash worlds were filled with spirits that lived in animals, in plants, and in natural forces such as thunder and lightning. The most powerful spirits were the First People—especially Kakunupmawa, the sun god and Humash, the earth goddess—who lived long before humans.

Chumash tradition says that the sun spirit travels the heavens every day, carrying a burning torch made of tree bark.

A bald eagle—sacred to many Native American peoples—soars through the sky.

Chumash Rock Paintings

The most mysterious expression of Chumash beliefs is found in paintings on cave walls and rock faces throughout their territory. Very little is known about these rock paintings. Some of them clearly show human and animal figures, but others are much stranger. They were probably painted for religious reasons, but nobody knows for certain, and it is possible that we never will.

Many of the locations of Chumash rock paintings are kept secret, so people cannot accidentally damage them. One of the few places where rock paintings can be seen by the public is Painted Cave State Historic Park, just a few miles north of Santa Barbara.

Strange, beautiful rock paintings are hidden away in caves like this one throughout Chumash territory.

One of many places sacred to the Chumash

At the end of his journey, the sun god shakes the torch to put out the flame. As he does this, he scatters sparks across the night sky, creating the stars.

The Chumash honored the spirits with many ceremonies and festivals. The most important occasions of the year were the harvest festival, which honored Humash after the acorns were gathered, and the **winter solstice** festival, which celebrated the "rebirth" of the sun spirit.

These religious celebrations were led by the *paxa*, the spiritual leader of a Chumash village. The *paxa*—who could be either a man or a woman—was helped by many **shamans**. Some shamans treated sick people with medicines made from plants, including elderberry and willow bark, and with carved stones that the Chumash believed could draw sickness out of a person's body. Other shamans were thought to be able to bring rain or good hunting and fishing. Chumash shamans sometimes took a powerful drug called **toloache**, which they believed gave them "visions" of the spirit world.

The children of the wealthiest Chumash families were invited to join a secret society called the *antap*. They performed sacred songs, dances, and rituals that honored the spirits. Members of the *antap* always stayed hidden behind wooden fences, so the ordinary Chumash could not see them.

4 · A CHANGING WORLD

When the twentieth century began, many Chumash traditions and beliefs were almost forgotten. Few people still spoke the Chumash language fluently, and very few "full-blooded" Chumash were left after years of intermarriage with other Native American peoples, and with Spanish and American settlers.

The remaining Chumash struggled—and continue to struggle—with many of the same problems that other Native American peoples face: poverty, unemployment, and alcohol and drug abuse. Even so, despite the many troubles they have experienced, the Chumash people and their remarkable culture are very much alive today.

Perhaps the first step in the "rebirth" of the Chumash came in 1901, when the U.S. government set aside seventy-

A Chumash mother and daughter

The Santa Ynez Reservation is located in Santa Barbara County, California.

five acres (thirty hectares) of land for the Santa Ynez Reservation. Not many Chumash actually live on the reservation, but those who do are the only Chumash recognized as a Native American people by the U.S. government. The

Santa Ynez Reservation has also been an important source of economic growth, especially since 2003, when a new resort and casino opened, bringing money and jobs to the Santa Ynez Valley.

Many historians and **anthropologists** study the Chumash. The most important institution for studying Chumash culture is the Santa Barbara Museum of Natural History on Mission Creek in the heart of traditional Chumash territory. The

The experts at the Santa Barbara Museum have helped to make the world aware of the greatness of Chumash culture.

The Chumash Language

The Chumash language may be part of the Hokan family of languages, spoken by Native American peoples in California and Mexico. There are at least five different dialects of Chumash. Here are a few words in the Inezeño dialect.

Chumash Word	Pronounced	English Translation
aqniwil	ak-NEE-will	to think
'alolk'oy	a-LOYK-koy	dolphin
haku	HA-koo	hello
milimol	mee-lee-MOL	mountain
sup	SHOOP	earth

museum has the finest collection of Chumash **artifacts** in the world, and researchers at the museum have spent many years studying the Chumash culture and language.

A researcher at the Santa Barbara Museum is also trying to help "find" the Chumash people. Since 1992 John Johnson

Visitors learn about Chumash traditions from a tour guide.

has been asking Chumash to give him **genetic** samples—hair or saliva—that he can compare with other people's DNA, or genetic information, and with ancient artifacts. His research is helping to identify people who have Chumash ancestry. It also shows connections between the Chumash and other Native American peoples who have lived as far away as Alaska and South America.

The people who have done the most to keep the old ways alive are the Chumash themselves. We owe much of what we know about them to a remarkable Chumash woman named Maria Solares, who was born sometime in the 1840s and died in 1923. She spent years working with **linguist** John P. Harrington, teaching him her language and telling him the myths of her people. Another very important Chumash figure was the shaman Semu Huaute ("Grandfather Semu"), who died in 2004 at the age of ninety-four. During his long life, he helped revive the traditional religious practices of the Chumash.

Today, many people are working hard to preserve the Chumash culture. The Wishtoyo Foundation, for example—named after the rainbow bridge that the Chumash believe they crossed long ago—studies and teaches the Chumash language. The foundation is also planning to build the Nicholas Canyon Demonstration Village, a working community that will show visitors what traditional Chumash life was like. Another excellent place to learn about the history and traditions of the Chumash is the Chumash Interpretive Center and Museum in Thousand Oaks.

The flags of the United States and the Chumash people fly together.

The sea life of the Pacific — like these bottlenose dolphins — have always been very important to the Chumash.

The Chumash are also reviving one of the most exciting parts of their way of life. In 1976 a group of Chumash paddled a tomol—the first one built in 134 years—from the mainland to the Channel Islands. Since then, Chumash paddlers have made the journey several more times. It is said that dolphins sometimes keep the paddlers company—perhaps welcoming their Chumash brothers and sisters back to their traditional home.

·TIME LINE

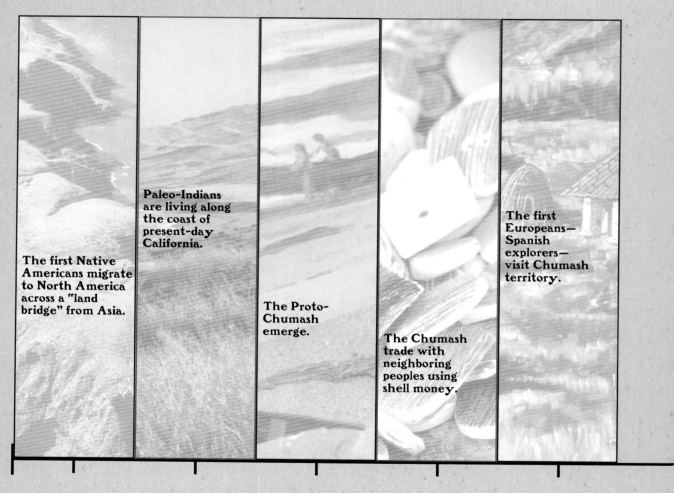

The first Native Americans migrate to North America across a "land bridge" from Asia.

Paleo-Indians are living along the coast of present-day California.

The Proto-Chumash emerge.

The Chumash trade with neighboring peoples using shell money.

The first Europeans—Spanish explorers—visit Chumash territory.

c 20,000 BCE   13,000 BCE   3000 BCE   1200 CE   1542

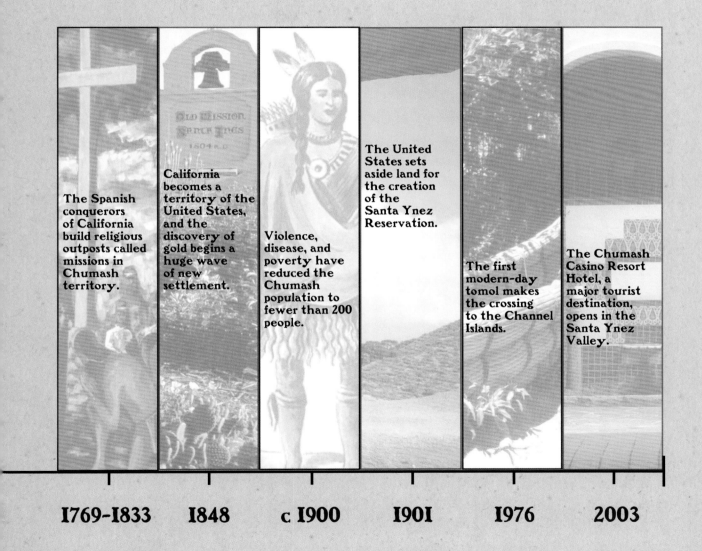

The Spanish conquerors of California build religious outposts called missions in Chumash territory.

California becomes a territory of the United States, and the discovery of gold begins a huge wave of new settlement.

Violence, disease, and poverty have reduced the Chumash population to fewer than 200 people.

The United States sets aside land for the creation of the Santa Ynez Reservation.

The first modern-day tomol makes the crossing to the Channel Islands.

The Chumash Casino Resort Hotel, a major tourist destination, opens in the Santa Ynez Valley.

1769-1833   1848   c 1900   1901   1976   2003

· GLOSSARY

anthropologists: Those who study the cultures of different peoples.

'aps: Dome-shaped Chumash houses.

artifacts: Things created by a people.

genetic: Referring to the hereditary characteristics, such as eye color, that make a person unique.

hereditary: Handed down from one generation of a family to the next.

linguist: Someone who studies languages.

migrate: To move from one part of the world to another.

Paleo-Indians: The earliest Native Americans.

Proto-Chumash: The ancestors of the Chumash.

shaman: Someone who is thought to practice magic or work with the spirit world.

steatite: A soft soapstone found in the Channel Islands and elsewhere.

temescal: A Chumash place for religious ceremonies; also called a sweat lodge.

tikauwich: A Native American game (also called shinny) in which players used sticks to knock a ball through goalposts.

toloache: A drug, made from a wild plant called jimsonweed, used by Chumash shamans.

tule: A water plant that grows in swampy areas in California.

winter solstice: The day of the year that has the least daylight.

• FIND OUT MORE

Books

Ansary, Mir Tamim. *California Indians*. Chicago: Heinemann Library, 2000.

Bial, Raymond. *The Chumash (Lifeways)*. New York: Benchmark Books, 2001.

Lee, Georgia. *A Day with a Chumash*. Minneapolis, MN: Runestone Press, 1999.

Sonneborn, Liz. *The Chumash*. Minneapolis, MN: Lerner Publications, 2007.

Young, Robert. *A Personal Tour of La Purisima*. Minneapolis, MN: Lerner Publications, 1999.

Web Sites

Chumash Indian Life: The Santa Barbara Museum of Natural History
www.sbnature.org/research/anthro/chumash/index.htm

Chumash Interpretive Center and Museum
www.chumashcenter.org/

Inezeño Vocabulary Illustrated
www.chumashlanguage.com/vocab/vocab-00-fr.html

Santa Ynez Band of Chumash Indians: Chumash History
www.santaynezchumash.org/history.html

Wishtoyo Foundation—Nicholas Canyon Demonstration Village
www.wishtoyo.org/projects-cultural-nicholas-canyon-demonstration-village.html

About the Author

Terry Allan Hicks has written more than a dozen titles for Benchmark Books, about everything from the common cold to the state of New Hampshire. He lives in Connecticut with his wife, Nancy, and their three sons, Jamie, Jack, and Andrew.

· INDEX

Page numbers in **boldface** are illustrations.